A Day on a Journey to Lakeside Shopping Mall

Parenting and Families
Volume 1
A-Z

SABINAH ADEWOLE

AuthorHouse™ UK
1663 Liberty Drive
Bloomington, IN 47403 USA
www.authorhouse.co.uk
UK TFN: 0800 0148641 (Toll Free inside the UK)
UK Local: 02036 956322 (+44 20 3695 6322 from outside the UK)

Because of the dynamic nature of the Internet, any web addresses or links contained in this book may have changed since publication and may no longer be valid. The views expressed in this work are solely those of the author and do not necessarily reflect the views of the publisher, and the publisher hereby disclaims any responsibility for them.

Any people depicted in stock imagery provided by Getty Images are models, and such images are being used for illustrative purposes only. Certain stock imagery © Getty Images.

This book is printed on acid-free paper.

ISBN: 978-1-6655-8805-8 (sc)
ISBN: 978-1-6655-8806-5 (e)

Print information available on the last page.

Published by AuthorHouse 04/12/2021

authorHOUSE®

Introduction

Sabinah Adewole is a bestselling author. She has enjoyed reading since she was a young child. She studied English, and her poetry has been informed from her experiences on her journeys of life, and it has inspired a lot of readers across the globe.

This book is her fourth children's book. In it she covers such themes as confidence, trust, bonding, family choices, identity, motherhood, fatherhood, and disability.

The poems in this series were mainly created in the United Kingdom on the author's journey to a shopping mall with her daughter when lockdown brought on by the COVID-19 pandemic was eased. It was an opportunity for children to enjoy a day out with their families during the summer break. This experience brought back childhood memories for both the author and her daughter as they observed the children in the shopping mall.

Her first children's poetry book, *A Child's Journey through Poetry* (Volume 1) was published in America in December 2019 and is a bestseller. Copies of her books are available in North America, Australia, and on many online platforms such as Booktopia, Biblio.Co.Uk, Waterstone.com, indigo.ca, and Book Depository.

Sabinah has been influenced by the various workshops in which she has participated. She has grown on the poetry circuit, promoting her poetry at various circuits. This has been evident in most of her poems.

Her poems are written in free-prose style, bringing out the truth and beauty in everyday living. Some of her poems are classified as haiku, epistolary, allusion, how-to poetry, object poetry, smell poetry, split or cento poetry, and ekphrastic poetry.

A Day on a Journey to Lakeside Shopping Mall

Volume 1
Parenting and Families

Dedication

This book is dedicated to my daughter Rebekah, who was part of the journey and inspiration of completing this book.

Contents

The Boy in the Neon T-Shirt

A dam is aged around 9,
Enjoying a day shopping with his dad.
A day like no other to me, an observer
with my daughter enjoying a coffee.
Adam inspired me to write about him.
The colour of his T-shirt is bold
And depicts confidence.
Adam seems a confident child.
Are you inspired by his journey?
What's your favourite colour?

Composed 25/8/2020

The Two Girls with the Backpacks

Bintu and Binta were enjoying a day out.
They were with Mum,
Standing by the pretzel stand.
Bintu and Binta are identical twins.
I could not tell one from the other.
They were dressed in the same clothing,
Pink top with jeans, and were carrying the same
Backpack.
But Binta wanted cinnamon on her pretzel,
While Bintu wanted hazelnuts on hers.
So the twins looked alike but had their choices and preferences.
What's your favourite choice of pretzel?

Composed 31/8/2020

2

The Boy and the Dad Pulling Down His Son's T-Shirt in the Mall

He was about 3, enjoying a day out.
Charlie and his dad were enjoying bonding.
He was a toddler and seemed to be getting bored.
We sat and watched from the distance in front of
Superdrug's.
He pulled at his top, trying to take it off.
His dad squatted to his level,
Spoke in a soft tone to reassure him.
Charlie became relaxed, let go of his T-shirt.

Dad held him close, and they carried on their journey.
Do you enjoy shopping?
Do you recall a time you went shopping with your dad?
What did you enjoy about the trip?

Composed 1/9/2020

3

The Little Girl Playing with Her Brother While Mum Breastfed

As we sat at the coffee shop, enjoying a day out,
A mum and her baby arrived.
The baby was about 6 months old, in a blue-and-white jumpsuit.
Mum sat across the room from us.
She started to breastfeed her baby.
She was about 19,
My daughter's age.
Few minutes later, a nan and daughters.
Aged about 5, arrived.
Danielle started to play with her brother,
Touching his head,
Pulling his ears,
Caressing his hand as Mum continued to breastfeed.
The nan joined in conversation.
It was such a delight to see a family enjoying a day out.
Have you seen a mum breastfeed before?
Have you a baby brother or sister?
We sat, watched, and carried on with our journey.

Composed 2/9/2020

4

The Baby Boy with Arms around His Head

It was a nice day in Lakeside.
The children were on vacation.
The mums and dads were enjoying the day;
The children were having fun;
The baby was in his mum's arms.
He was about 6 months old.
Edward was a cute baby.
He was dressed in his jumpsuit.
He had his arms around his head.
That drew my attention to him in his mum's arms.

She sat, and I just looked on and later looked away
And carried on where I stopped.
What has caught your attention in the mall?
Did you stop to watch, or did you carry on walking?
The baby in his mother's arms.

Composed 4/9/2020

5

The Girl Pulling at Her Mum's Hand

Freya was about 6.
   She was enjoying a day shopping,
Bonding with Mum.
I was doing the same with my daughter.
I have always had lovely memories of
Coming to Lakeside,
Doing my Christmas shopping.
But on this day, I was here
Bonding with my daughter.
The little girl reminded me of me
When my daughter was much younger.
She came to see Father Christmas.

I thought the girl had had enough
And just wanted to leave
And carry on her journey.
Mum carried on walking.
How many times have you seen this happen
On a day out?

Composed 6/9/2020

6

The Little Boy in the Wheelchair Coming Down the Escalator with Mum and Dad

As we sat at the eating area,
We could see the top of the escalator.
We could see the traffic going up and down
As we enjoyed our coffee,
Bonding with my daughter
Over a pretzel.
George seemed about 3 years of age,
Sleeping as Mum and Dad held tight to the handles.
As they descended, he woke up,
Seemed a bit startled.
Mum was on hand to reassure him.

She gave him a book,
An iPad, and he seemed happy.
As they got to the end of the ride,
Our eyes met.
George smiled, and I returned his smile.
His smile made a difference to my day.
Have your eyes met someone, and you felt amused or
Thought, *What a nice way to end my coffee,*
Like I thought?

Composed 8/9/2020

7

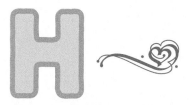

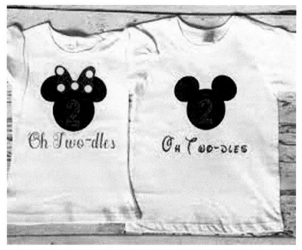

The Two Boys in the Mickey Mouse T-Shirts with Mum and Nan

Harry and Howard were both 5.
They were enjoying a day out
With Mum and Nan.
It was the school summer break,
The kids out of school since March,
The children all having fun.
I spotted them as they had Mickey Mouse
T-shirts on.
They reminded me of Disneyland Paris.
They brought back nice memories for me.
It's amazing how a little image can do wonders
For anyone.
Harry and Howard went into the toy shop.

It was their fifth birthday.
What does Mickey Mouse remind you of?

Composed 10/9/2020

The Girl in the White Cropped Top and Skater Skirt

It was a nice summer's day.
Lots of shoppers in the mall.
People generally having a good day.
Nice atmosphere.
Sitting with my daughter in Starbucks,
Enjoying a coffee and pretzel,
Chatting and laughing.
The young girl in a cropped top
Stood out in the crowd.
She had on a cropped top and white skirt.
My daughter said, 'Skater skirt'.
I'd never heard of that before.
We learn something every day.

I thought I would write about it
Then and called it
'The Girl in the White Cropped Top and a
Skater Skirt'.
Indigo was about 9 and had skates on.
Have you a pair of skate shoes?
I bought my daughter a pair before
She went ice skating with her friends.
Have you been skating before?

Composed 16/9/2020

The Girl in the Jeans Jacket with Her Mum, also Wearing a Jean Jacket

June was out with Mum
  The pair on their day
Looked amazing to see.
A mum and her daughter
In the same outfit—
Matching colours,
Matching outfits
With a butterfly.
I once remember
Wearing the same outfit
With my mother.
Just the once,
On her fiftieth birthday.
It was the one and only time

I can remember.
It now seems special
To trigger a memory for me,
The mum and her daughter.
Have you matched outfits before?
My two sons matched outfits
For so long when they were
Young.
Have you a memory of when you matched
Outfits?
And who was it you matched with?

Composed 18/9/20

10

K

The Boy with the Adidas Hood and His Sister

In the midst of the crowd
On the second floor,
As we strolled along looking
Through the shop windows,
Was this little boy of about 3
With his older sister.
Kieran appeared tired.
Had his hood on in the mall.
My daughter grew up in tracksuits;
He reminded me of her.
She loved her track bottoms.
The boy was not enjoying his day.
But his top stood out,

With the stripes and the Adidas logo.
I guess also because he had his hood on.
What is your best outfit?
Does this remind you of the gym?
Or remind you of playing a sport?
Or remind you of gangs, as hoods
Are associated with gangs?
What are your thoughts?

Composed 20/9/2020

11

The Boy with the Shopping Bag and Lanyard

It was in the mall in Lakeside.
We sat at the food court
On the second floor.
We had the famous Primark store,
Which had three floors of bargain
Shopping, nice quality.
We saw a boy of about 6
Carrying a Primark bag.
He had a lanyard on his neck.
He caught my attention, as he seemed lost
And was looking around.
Leon appeared lost,
But that was my assumption.

His mum had gone to the bathroom.
He was waiting for her to return.
It is not always what we perceive.
Sometimes our minds play tricks.
We need to focus on the here and now.
Leon was safe and enjoying a day out.
The Primark bag considered the environment,
As all other shops' bags were nylon.
I thought that was fab to see.

Composed on 24/9/2020

The Asian Couple with Their Son in the Buggy and Daughter

They struck me as a nice couple.
The family orientation,
The Asian-looking couple
With their young son of about 3
And their daughter,
Enjoying a day out.
But what was striking was even though
They were a young family,
They could still show their love in public.
Madison was sitting up in the buggy,
And his sister was looking in his eyes.
They were playful and enjoying each other's
Company.

Do you enjoy spending time together
As a family? As a couple?
As siblings?
Do you enjoy each other's company?

Composed 27/9/2020

The Girl with the Panda

Enjoying a day out
Amongst the crowd
In the mall,
The girl stood out with her panda.
She was cuddling it in her arms.
She stood out like a kite.
Her panda was black and white.
She seemed oblivious to her surroundings,
Playing away as she walked along.
She was aged about 6.
Naomi was of mixed heritage,
A pleasure to watch.
When next you are in a mall,

Would you look out for the next panda?
Or for the next kite?

Composed 4/10/2020

14

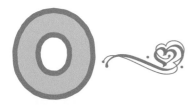

The Two Girls with Masks and Their Parents

There was a pandemic.
We had to social distance and stay two metres apart.
But what was interesting was that children did not have to wear masks.
I had seen a number of children without masks on.
So to see these two girls aged about 5 and 6
Wearing their masks and having fun in the mall
With their parents caught my attention.
I liked the fact that they were oblivious to the fact that other children
Didn't have them on, but they were confident and felt safe to have them on in public.
I thought the pandemic was food for thought for everyone.
We all had to be safe and protect each other.
If a child who did not need to do this
Could do this, then we as adults had to do the same,
Safely social distancing.
Orange and Ohio pulled this off nicely
With their parents in the mall.

Composed 6/10/2020

15

The Boy in the Red T-Shirt and His Cap

The colour red has always been an eye-catcher.
Red is one of the colours that goes well with my skin tone.
Would I say it's my favourite colour?
Not really, but I enjoy wearing a red dress to a Valentine's Day event.
I recall standing out in the crowd.
So when I saw Prince in his red T-shirt,
It was not surprising he stood out in the crowd.
He had a red hat on to match his T-shirt.
It reminded me of the Bible passage,
"Let your light shine so they can see your good works

And praise your father in heaven".
Prince could not be hidden in the crowd in the mall.
His red T-shirt made him stand out.
I hope we can all stand out in the crowd too.
He appeared stylish in matching colours.
Do you remember standing out in college or at a party or in a shopping mall?
The boy in the red T-shirt and cap just did,
And so could you.

Composed 8/10/2020

The Girl with the Alice Band and Her Black Parents

Do you recall visiting a mall with Mum and Dad?
Do you recall entering the shops with Mum and Dad?
How did that make you feel?
Are you a daddy's girl or a mummy's girl?
Are you closer to your dad?
The beauty of shopping as a family is entertaining.
It could lead to bonding with each other.
I saw the Black couple with their daughter,
Their princess, their queen.
They were a family having a fun day out.

I was out with my daughter,
Enjoying a day too.
You could also spend time bonding as a single parent with your child.
Shopping is bonding time for some.

Composed 10/10/20

The Boy in the Striped T-Shirt

Have you ever met anyone with an infectious smile?
Have you ever met anyone who is always happy?
Have you ever been in a happy state of mind?
How does that make you feel?
Do you transfer that energy to people around you
In the room at the time?
When you look at people who are happy,
It triggers a chemical in your brain.
You realise you begin to smile back at yourself
Or the person who started the smile.
It creates a ripple effect in our society.
Robert had a big smile on his face when I saw him in the mall.
He drew attention to himself.
He made me and my daughter smile.
We were delighted to see someone with a smile on their face.
He made a difference in the mall.
Be happy.

Composed 11/10/2020

The Girl in the Red T-shirt and Nike Trainer Pushing the Buggy walking with Mum

Have you ever had to try on your dad's or mum's shoes?
Have you had to try on your mum's high heels or your dad's boots?
These are all very familiar actions you may have performed.
A girl would wear her mum's make-up and check herself out in the mirror.
A boy would try on his dad's shirts and make it look like overalls.
These are all familiar acts.
Have you ever wondered why this happens?
Children play with their dolls and connect with their maternal sides.
This was so peculiar when I saw the girl pushing the buggy in the mall.
She seemed to derive pleasure from this task.
I decided to call her Samantha, as she reminded me of a family friend's daughter called Samantha.
She always had her doll with her whenever she came round my house.
I always played with a doll as a child.

I had a doll and she would make noises.
Have you ever seen a Black doll?
The girl pushing the buggy triggered memories.
My daughter's godmother bought her a Black woven doll before.
I am not sure if my daughter liked her doll very much.
Samantha was about 6 years of age.

Composed 13/10/2020

The Chinese Boy in the Polo Shirt and His Sister and Parents

The boy struck me in the crowd.
    As a child, when I was growing up, I was very shy.
I could not enter a room full of people.
I do not know how I overcame my shyness,
But it stayed with me for a long time.
This is why when I saw the Chinese boy and his family,
It reminded me of my childhood.
They were all dressed in matching colours.
This was intriguing, and this showed unity
Within the family setting.
When a child feels accepted within a family
And is shown love, this helps the child grow and develop.
Do you recall a time you felt this way in your family—
Shy, loved, and united?
Tommy must have felt very special.
Did this family trigger anything for you?

Composed 15/10/2020

U

The Boy and Girl in Printed Masks and Their Dad

When I was growing up,
We took pride in matching fabrics.
The whole family would wear the same material.
This was during special occasions,
Like Christmas or Easter.
But this has become a popular tradition.
Now you can wear matching fabrics for many
Parties or celebrations.
So whenever I see matching fabrics in masks,
It triggers a memory for me as a child.
It looked amazing to see the family in
Printed masks, all matching,
Keeping safe, and maintaining distance.

The joy of being together was not overshadowed.
The zebra colours, black and white,
Were very striking.
It made such a difference to see such creativity in
Masking within a family.
The boy was called Urela and the girl Ursula.
The disposable masks litter our streets.
Do you have a printed, washable mask?
What's your favourite mask?
Your favourite could help the environment.

Composed 16/10/2020

The Girl in Black Standing in the Queue with Her Dad and Brother

She was about 6,
Standing and staring,
In black from head to toe,
Quite unusual, as it was summer.
Her dad and brother standing alongside her in the queue into
Primark it seemed.
I have always thought of goths as young adults,
But she was a child of about 6.
She already had her style, which may appear
Ludicrous.
But that was her,
Black lipstick and all,

Dark hair and dark jewellery.
She reminded me of the cartoon
In *Wicked.*
I was taken aback, as all the other kids were in different but bright colours.
She was Vivian, and her brother was called Tony for short.
They aren't twins, I thought.
But then they could be,
But such a nonidentical pair.
Vivian and Tony.

Composed 20/10/2020

23

The Girl in the Printed Jumpsuit with Her Parents in the Changing Area

Do you recall a time visiting a mall as a child,
Waiting with your mum in the changing area,
Trying to try on new clothing to see
If it was the right fit for the occasion?

Do you recall a time visiting a mall
With your mum trying to find your school uniforms?
I recall travelling with my daughter to central London
To buy her school uniform in John Lewis.

Do you recall a time visiting the mall as a child
With your dad, and he had to use the bathroom,
But because you were little, you had to wait outside,
Or he had to leave you with a stranger?

Do you recall visiting a mall
With Dad and Mum, and your little sibli
Had to have their nappie changed
In the stick-out bed on the wall?

Do you recall visiting the mall as a child,
Mum in the restroom,
You waiting outside the door,
Dancing away at the mirror.

The little girl in the jumpsuit
Just reminded me of that.
Her name was Warrior Woman.

Composed 21/10/2020

24

The Little Girl in White with Her Mum and Pink Bag

I always liked white as a child.
Memories of my white dress on a Sunday walk
To town in boarding school,
Or my white dress when I was baptised
In River Jordan as an adult.
My white shirt under my green pinafore
In secondary school.
The little girl in white amongst so many shoppers
In the mall with her mum
Reminded me of an angel.

I felt the connection between mum and daughter.
She seemed like an angel of peace
Amongst the hustle and bustle in the mall.
She was a ray of sunshine, I thought.
What does the colour white mean to you?
What does white signify to you?
Does it bring up any memories?
Alexandra was a suitable name, I felt,
As I could not think of a name with X.

Composed 22/10/2020

The Mixed-Race Girl out Shopping with Her Mother

I know that feeling of spending time with your daughter,
Or spending time with family or siblings.
I was out shopping with my daughter
When I caught this image.
It's ironic, as I was doing the exact thing.
I was writing my own story, I guess,
Except my daughter was much older.
But it does not change the emotion—
The treasures of life,
Wanting to gain trust,
Wanting to have those memories.

I guess I did not get to have these memories as a child.
I was too young when I moved to live with family and cousins.
The mixed-race girl triggered memories of joy and happiness.
Her name was Yasmine.

Composed 24/10/20

The Little Boy in the Buggy Swinging His Feet

Zack was enjoying a day out with Mum and Dad.
He must have been about 3.
Mum had forgotten Zack on the queue
As she went off towards the till to pay.
I noticed Zack swinging his feet.
He caught my attention with his feet.
He was drawing attention as he looked towards
His mum; his dad was in another shop altogether.
I thought, *What a wonderful day he has had!*
Mum suddenly realised she had left Zack behind.
She ran across the shop to fetch him.

So sometimes we should not assume a child is throwing
A tantrum or seeking attention, because that could exactly be
The case to help him or her, who may be in trouble.
Have you ever been forgotten in a shop in the mall
Or in the park or library?
It got me thinking, *Did you feel safe or feel alone?*
How did that make you feel?

Composed 27/10/2020

27

Testimonials

"She gives each poem a particular spin; some bear a resemblance to sonnets, others remind me of concrete poetry. The words themselves are used to create imagery or feeling."

"I feel as if the writer is dancing through life and inviting the reader to join in."

"Her poetry is optimistic, motivational, and heart-warming. The poems are about her travels and personal experiences."

"She is clearly a world traveller and poetically narrates her trips to various places "

"Her writing is very interesting and well acknowledged on the international circuit."

About the Book

A Day on a Journey to Lakeside Shopping Mall, *Volume 1,* is about a day the author and her daughter spent in a shopping mall. Children were enjoying a day during the summer holidays after the first lockdown during the pandemic. She thought to showcase memories of her childhood and her daughter's childhood through the children they saw in the mall. I guess this is relevant for any child enjoying a day of shopping during a school holiday in the shopping mall.

Each poem identifies with an alphabet letter to make them interesting and engaging while helping children learn the message in the poem. This book exposes different elements of a child's journey and their different phases on their journeys. These elements include confidence, trust, bonding, family choice, motherhood, disability and love.

The author has taken a common event -going shopping- and turned into an enjoyable learning experience for the Child/Children.

This book is for all age groups who may find it brings up enjoyable memories and reflections such as when they were young and doing similar things with their families, such as dressing alike on special occasions or for that Christmas photograph every year.

Printed in the United States
by Baker & Taylor Publisher Services